FamilyFun's Cookies for Christmas

EDITED BY
DEANNA F. COOK
AND THE EXPERTS AT
FamilyFun Magazine

FamilyFun's
Cookies
for Christmas

EDITORS
Deanna F. Cook and
Alexandra Kennedy

MANAGING EDITOR
Priscilla Totten

COPY EDITORS
Susan Roberts and
Mike Trotman

EDITORIAL ASSISTANTS
Nicole Blasenak,
Jean Graham, and
Debra Liebson

CREATIVE DIRECTOR
Hans Teensma,
Impress, Inc.

DESIGNER
Carolyn Eckert

ART DIRECTOR
David Kendrick

PICTURE EDITOR
Mark Mantegna

PHOTOGRAPHY
Jade Albert, Michael
Carroll, Peter N. Fox,
Tom Hopkins, Becky
Luigart-Stayner, and
Shaffer/Smith Photography

PRODUCTION
Martha Jenkins and
Jennifer Mayer

**TECHNOLOGY
COORDINATOR**
Luke Jaeger

**CONTRIBUTING
EDITORS**
Jonathan Adolph,
Ann Hallock, Cindy A.
Littlefield, and Vivi
Mannuzza

This book is dedicated to *FamilyFun*'s avid bakers everywhere.

Many of the ideas in this book were adapted from articles in *FamilyFun* magazine. *FamilyFun* is a division of the Walt Disney Publishing Group. To order a subscription, call 800-289-4849.

The staffs of *FamilyFun* and Impress, Inc., conceived and produced *FamilyFun's Cookies for Christmas* at 244 Main Street, Northampton, MA 01060, in collaboration with Hyperion, 114 Fifth Avenue, New York, NY 10011.

ISBN 0-7868-6469-9

Printed by Worzalla Publishing Co., Stevens Point, WI.

Special thanks to the following *FamilyFun* magazine writers for their wonderful recipes: Barbara Albright, Lynne Bertrand, Cynthia Caldwell, Dorothy Foltz-Gray, Mollie Katzen, and Emily B. Todd. We also would like to thank the models and the following stylists: Bonnie Anderson/Team, Grace Arias, Susan Fox, Marie Piraino, and Stacey Webb.

We also extend our gratitude to *FamilyFun*'s many creative readers who shared with us their ideas for baking with their families. We have credited them by name.

This book would not have been possible without the talented *FamilyFun* magazine staff, who edited and art-directed many of these recipes for the magazine from 1993 to 1998. We also would like to thank our partners at Hyperion, especially Bob Miller, Wendy Lefkon, Kris Kliemann, David Lott, Lisa Kitei, and Robin Friedman.

About our major contributors:
Deanna F. Cook is a Senior Editor of *FamilyFun* and the author of *FamilyFun's Cookbook* and *FamilyFun's Crafts,* both from Hyperion, and *The Kids' Multicultural Cookbook* and *Kids' Pumpkin Projects* from Williamson. She develops recipes in her Northampton, Massachusetts, kitchen with the help of her daughter, Ella Skye, and a bunch of neighborhood kids.

Barbara Albright is the former Editor in Chief of *Chocolatier,* and the coauthor of *Completely Cookies, Mostly Muffins, Quick Chocolate Fixes, Cooking with Regis & Kathy Lee,* and *Girl Food.* Her daughter, Samantha, and son, Stone, are her official taste-testers.

Emily B. Todd, a regular contributor to *Family Fun,* has baked gingerbread men every Christmas Eve since she was eight — using the same treasured cookie cutter. She lives in Chicago with her husband.

Cynthia Caldwell is a food stylist and writer who develops many of the recipes that appear in *FamilyFun.* She lives in Whately, Massachusetts, with her husband, Shawn, and two young children, Isabelle and Russell.

First edition
10 9 8 7 6 5 4 3 2 1

Table of Contents

Introduction

WHEN YOU HAVE FRESHLY BAKED Christmas cookies, you always have friends. Your kids line up to decorate gingerbread men, and neighbors stop by for Snowballs and mugs of hot chocolate. Even the dog seems to know when sugar cookies are coming out of the oven. It's a wonder there are any cookies left to put out for Santa.

Fortunately, there are plenty of Christmas cookies to go around in my house. As the food editor of *FamilyFun* magazine, it's my job to test dozens of cookie recipes for our special holiday issue each year. Once I've developed a recipe, I enlist the help of the kids in my neighborhood or the crew at my daughter's day-care center to give it a trial run. After an afternoon of baking, there are lots of sweet leftovers for the taste-testers — parents, friends, colleagues, and even Tony, my eighty-year-old neighbor who lives across the street.

To pass the *FamilyFun* recipe test, a cookie has to taste good. But it also should be simple enough for a busy parent to bake. Ideally, it should have steps that involve the kids

THE RULES OF COOKIE BAKING

* Put flour, sugar, butter, and other baking supplies on your holiday list. That way, you won't have to make a dozen trips to the store.
* Brush up on your baking skills. Read "Cookie Baking 101" on page 7 before you start.
* Add to your cookie cutter collection. Be sure you have cookie sheets, tins, plastic wrap, and other supplies, too.
* Try not to bake cookies without your kids. It may be easier on your own, but they'll miss out on the fun.
* When baking holiday cookies, listen to Christmas carols. It will put you in the holiday spirit — and provide a break in the busy season.

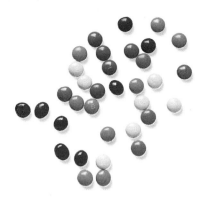

and variations that bring out your creativity. Our Best-ever Sugar Cookie dough,
for instance, can be flavored, decorated, and cut into cookies of any shape you like. The
recipes that go over best with kids, I've discovered, are playful. A cookie can be more
than a dessert — it can be a snowman, a cottage, or an ornament for the holiday tree.

In the pages of this book, you'll find the best Christmas cookie recipes that have
appeared in *FamilyFun* magazine from 1993 to 1998. Every year our readers and
staff members get into the holiday spirit by baking them with their kids. We hope you,
too, will try them this Christmas and discover those recipes that will become holiday
traditions for your family. *Merry Christmas!*

— *Deanna F. Cook*

* **Let the cookie chef take the first bite. Young chefs feel proud of their creations.**
* **Always share cookies with teachers, neighbors, and cousins. A gift from the kitchen tastes better and** means more than a gift from the mall.
* **Keep your cookie jar full. Around the holidays, have lots of sweets (and milk or tea) on hand for guests.**
* **Start an annual tradition.** Bake with your kids this Christmas and make it part of your holiday ritual.
* **Don't forget to leave cookies for Santa on Christmas Eve (and carrots for the reindeer).**

Best-ever Sugar Cookies

Best-ever Sugar Cookies

THIS MASTER RECIPE from *FamilyFun* contributor Barbara Albright makes sugar cookie dough that is strong enough for little hands to roll, sculpt, and cut with cookie cutters. Plus, it's versatile. Barbara found a way to turn it into all the playful sugar cookies in this book.

3½	cups all-purpose flour
½	teaspoon salt
1	cup unsalted butter, softened
⅔	cup sugar
1	large egg
1	tablespoon light corn syrup
1	tablespoon vanilla extract

In a medium-size bowl, mix the flour and salt. In a large bowl, cream the butter and sugar, stir in the egg, then the corn syrup and vanilla extract. One third at a time, add the flour mixture until thoroughly mixed. Pat the dough into two disks, wrap them in plastic, and refrigerate for 1 to 2 hours, or until firm enough to roll. If the dough is too firm, soften at room temperature for about 5 minutes.

Preheat the oven to 375°. Roll the dough to a ¼-inch thickness between two pieces of waxed paper or plastic wrap. Remove the top sheet of waxed paper and cut out the cookies with cookie cutters. Using a spatula, transfer the shapes to an ungreased baking sheet, leaving about 1 inch between the cookies. Bake for 8 to 10 minutes, or until the cookies start to brown lightly around the edges.

Set the baking sheet on a wire rack and cool for about 5 minutes. Transfer the cookies to racks and cool completely. The cookies can be stored in an airtight container in the freezer for up to 1 month and for up to 3 days at room temperature before you frost them. Makes 12 to 50 cookies, depending on their size.

Chocolate Sugar Cookies: After the last third of flour has been added to the dough, mix in 1 ounce melted, slightly cooled unsweetened chocolate.

Lemon Sugar Cookies: For a lemon surprise, add 1 teaspoon grated lemon peel or ½ teaspoon lemon extract.

Almond Sugar Cookies: Stir in ½ teaspoon almond extract.

Colorful Sugar Cookies: Page 9
Striped Cookies: Page 35

Prep Time: 20 minutes, plus baking. **Kids' Steps:** Helping to mix the dough and cutting it into shapes with cookie cutters.

cookie baking 101

* Bring all ingredients to room temperature.
* Use a glass measuring cup for all liquids. Spoon flour into a dry measuring cup and level with a knife.
* Check the oven temperature accuracy with an oven thermometer.
* Roll cookie dough between two sheets of waxed paper (so extra flour won't get incorporated). Cut cookies from edge to center.
* Bake cookies on the center rack in your oven for even browning.
* To avoid overbaked cookies, check them a few minutes before the minimum baking time and recheck every minute. Cool for 5 minutes, then transfer to a rack.
* Never put cookie dough on a hot baking sheet; the cookies will spread out too much.
* Don't run hot baking sheets under cold water. Abrupt temperature changes cause them to warp.

Choo-Choo Cookie Train

IF YOU MAKE this cookie train with a group of children, let each child decorate a car, then hitch the cookies together with shoestring licorice.

> **Best-ever Sugar Cookie dough (see page 7), colored or plain**
> **Lightweight cardboard**
> **Cookie Frosting (see page 15)**
> **Life Savers candies**
> **Shoestring licorice**
> **Edible passengers, such as ginger-bread men or gummy animals**
> **Edible cargo, such as pretzel logs**

Cut train templates about 2 by 3½ inches out of the cardboard to look like the cars above. Set on the rolled-out cookie dough. With the point of a sharp knife (parents only), cut out the cars. Bake as directed. Using frosting, attach Life Savers candies for wheels. Connect the cars with licorice and dabs of frosting. Add edible passengers and freight. Makes 30 cars.

Prep Time: 30 minutes, plus preparing and baking the Best-ever Sugar Cookie dough.
Kids' Steps: Mixing and rolling the cookie dough and decorating the train with candies.

COLORFUL SUGAR COOKIES

A dab of food coloring turns the Best-ever Sugar Cookie dough on page 7 into colorful sweets like this Choo-Choo Train. For vibrant colored cookies, simply divide the dough into portions and use a toothpick to add food coloring paste (available at party supply stores) to each one. Alternatively, add liquid food coloring, drop by drop, until you reach the desired hue. Knead the dough until the color is evenly distributed. For a flavor surprise, add ½ teaspoon of lemon extract to yellow dough, mint extract to green dough, and strawberry extract to red dough.

The Gingerbread Clan

The Gingerbread Clan

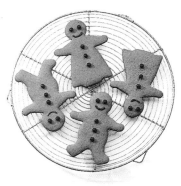

To a child, a gingerbread man is no ordinary cookie — he's a celebrity, a star in a legendary tale, an edible doll that can be made with flour and dressed in candy buttons. It's no wonder that kids love to bake one after another. Read a library version of the old English folktale "The Gingerbread Man" aloud, then invite your kids to roll and cut the dough into shapes, and cover their baked cookies with icing and candies.

4½	cups all-purpose flour
1	tablespoon ground cinnamon
2	teaspoons ground ginger
¼	teaspoon ground cloves
1¼	teaspoons baking soda
½	cup butter, softened
½	cup packed brown sugar
2	large eggs
¾	cup molasses

Red hots and shoestring licorice
Cookie Frosting (see page 15)

In a medium-size bowl, sift the flour, cinnamon, ginger, cloves, and baking soda. Set aside. In a large bowl, cream the butter and brown sugar with a wooden spoon or electric mixer. Add the eggs, one at a time, and then the molasses. Slowly add the flour mixture to the molasses mixture, stirring after each addition with the wooden spoon or mixer (the dough should be stiff).

Divide the dough in half, flatten into a thick pancake, and cover with plastic wrap. Refrigerate for 2 hours, or until firm enough to roll (if the dough becomes too stiff, soften for 10 minutes at room temperature for easy rolling).

Preheat the oven to 350°. Dust the counter generously with flour, roll out the dough to a ¼-inch thickness (alternatively, roll out the dough between two sheets of waxed paper). Use cookie cutters to cut out gingerbread men and a spatula to transfer them to a greased cookie sheet, spacing them 1 inch apart. Bake for 10 minutes, or until light brown.

Once the gingerbread men have cooled, invite your kids to add red hots and frosting features by squeezing cookie frosting through a pastry bag fitted with a writer's tip. Store away from any foxes who might snatch them up. Makes about 25 cookies.

Prep Time: 20 minutes, plus chilling, baking, and decorating. **Kids' Steps:** Measuring ingredients, mixing, rolling, and cutting the dough, and decorating the cookies.

> **Run, run, run as fast as you can. You can't catch me, I'm the gingerbread man!**
>
> —"The Gingerbread Man," an old English folktale

Celebration Sticks

FAMILYFUN READER Sarah Rose-marino, age eight, of North Canton, Ohio, dipped pretzels into a bowl of leftover melted chocolate, and this festive treat was born. For quick Christmas gifts, make the treats with white chocolate and red and green sprinkles.

1   cup semisweet chocolate chips
     (white or regular)
10   8-inch pretzel rods
Colored sprinkles

Melt the chocolate in the top of a double boiler or microwave in a bowl for 1 minute (watch closely — chips can burn easily in the microwave).

Dip the pretzels in the melted chocolate or use a plastic picnic knife to spread them with the chocolate. Roll in a bowl of sprinkles and dry on waxed paper. Makes 10.

Prep Time: 10 minutes. **Kids' Steps: Dipping the pretzels in the melted chocolate and rolling them in the sprinkles.**

Advent Calendar

AFTER WE RAN the directions for making this cookie Advent calendar in *FamilyFun* magazine, a record number of our readers counted down the days before Christmas one cookie at a time.

25 3- to 4-inch Best-ever Sugar
Cookies (see page 7), colored and
baked
Cookie Frosting (see page 15)
25 sandwich-size plastic bags
Ribbon or raffia
20- by 30-inch dish towel
25-inch-long dowel
30 safety pins

Write the numbers 1 to 25 on the cookies with frosting. Place each cookie in a plastic bag and tie with a ribbon. Set the towel, front side down, on your work surface with the dowel across the top of the towel. Fold the top edge over the dowel and secure with safety pins. Arrange the cookies on the front of the towel, evenly spaced, then pin in place. For a handle, tie a long piece of ribbon to each end of the dowel and hang within reach of the countdown team. Makes 25 cookies.

Prep Time: 45 minutes, plus baking the cookies.
Kids' Steps: Writing the numbers on the cookies with frosting, placing them in the plastic bags, and pinning the bags on the calendar.

Cookie-Decorating Party

Cookie-Decorating Party

LIKE SOME FANCIFUL PARTY hosted by Betty Crocker and Pablo Picasso, a cookie-decorating celebration lets kids and parents make treats and be merry. With a mountain of baked cookies, frosting, and decorations at hand, guests can roll up their sleeves and design cookie masterpieces, from candy-nosed reindeer to ornate holiday bells. At the end of the party, set up a show of all the artists' creations for everyone to admire and, of course, sample with tall glasses of milk.

Party Preparation

* This party is not exactly sugar-free, so you might want to invite guests to come after lunch or dinner. Send invitations (or telephone) a few weeks in advance.
* A week before the party, mix up batches of Best-ever Sugar Cookie dough (see page 7) and The Gingerbread Clan dough (see page 11). Form into disks, tightly wrap in foil or plastic, and freeze until ready to roll, cut, and bake.
* A few days before the party, defrost the dough and cut out and bake a variety of shapes to provide empty "canvases."
* On the day of the party, set up a child-size table for preschoolers and a card or kitchen table for bigger kids and adults. To prevent frosting disasters, cover your floor and counters with newspapers or a plastic drop cloth and have smocks on hand for draping the children.
* Assemble tubes of store-bought icing and/or assorted colors of Cookie Frosting (see recipe at right) in disposable pastry bags fitted with writing or star tips. Fill nonbreakable bowls with sprinkles, M&M's, jelly beans, gumdrops, red hots, chocolate chips, fruit leather, and other cookie decorations.
* Have ready a stack of damp paper towels for wiping hands and paper plates for holding the finished cookies.

Party Planning

* When the guests arrive, beckon them into your kitchen for cookie decorating.
* Let the kids decorate five cookies apiece.
* Award candy canes or other prizes for the goofiest, tallest, or most colorful creation. Then, arrange the entries on a platter and set on the table with the other cookies for all to admire.
* Wrap up any uneaten cookies for party favors.

cookie frosting

This basic frosting can be spread with a knife or squeezed through a pastry bag onto sugar cookies. If you plan to pipe the frosting through the bag, make it stiffer by adding a little less milk.

- 2 cups sifted confectioners' sugar
- 1/4 cup unsalted butter, softened
- 1/2 teaspoon vanilla extract
- 1 to 2 tablespoons milk
  Liquid or paste food coloring (optional)

in a large bowl and using an electric mixer set at low speed, beat the confectioners' sugar, butter, and vanilla extract until it reaches spreading consistency. Add more sugar or a little milk, if necessary, to achieve the right texture. Stir in the food coloring until combined, if desired. Makes about 1 1/2 cups.

Penny Snickerdoodles

IF YOU HAVE a house full of kids, these coin-size cinnamon-sugar cookies won't last long in your cookie jar. For more than one bite per cookie, make regular Snickerdoodles — simply roll larger pieces of dough and increase the baking time.

1⅓ cups all-purpose flour
1 teaspoon cream of tartar
½ teaspoon baking soda
⅛ teaspoon salt
½ cup unsalted butter, softened
¾ cup plus 2 tablespoons sugar
1 large egg
2 teaspoons cinnamon

Preheat the oven to 400°. In a medium-size bowl, sift the flour, cream of tartar, baking soda, and salt. In a large bowl, cream the butter and ¾ cup of sugar. Stir in the egg until thoroughly blended. One third at a time, stir in the dry ingredients until thoroughly mixed.

Pinch off small pieces of dough and roll into balls the size of marbles (a fun job for kids). On a plate or in a shallow bowl, mix the cinnamon and 2 tablespoons of sugar. Roll the balls in the cinnamon-sugar mixture and place on an ungreased cookie sheet 2 inches apart. Flatten the cookies with the bottom of a glass or jar (dip it into the cinnamon-sugar mixture to keep it from sticking).

Bake the cookies for 6 to 10 minutes, or until lightly browned along the edges. Transfer to a cooling rack. When they're thoroughly cool, store in an airtight jar. Makes 10 to 12 dozen cookies.

Prep Time: 30 minutes, plus baking time.
Kids' Steps: Measuring and mixing the cookie dough, rolling it into balls, and covering it in the cinnamon sugar.

Penny Snickerdoodles

Giant M&M Cookie Pops

FRESH-BAKED M&M cookies may hit the spot after school, but when the treats are baked on a stick and tied with a ribbon, every kid in your child's class will want one for Christmas.

2¼ cups all-purpose flour
1 teaspoon baking powder
½ teaspoon salt
1 cup unsalted butter, softened
1 cup sugar
½ cup packed light brown sugar
2 large eggs
2 teaspoons vanilla extract

2 cups red and green M&M's, or chocolate or peanut butter chips
15 Popsicle sticks (see page 51)

In a medium-size bowl, mix the flour, baking powder, and salt. In a large bowl, cream the butter and sugars, then beat in the eggs, one at a time. Stir in the vanilla extract. Gradually mix in the flour mixture. Stir in the M&M's. For chewier cookies, refrigerate the dough overnight.

Preheat the oven to 300°. Using a ⅓-cup measure (for giant cookies) or ¼-cup measure (for monster cookies), drop the dough about 3 inches apart onto ungreased baking sheets. Insert a Popsicle stick, at least 1 inch deep, into each one to form a pop. Bake for 30 to 35 minutes, or until light brown. Set the sheet on a wire rack and cool for 5 minutes. Using a metal spatula, transfer the cookies to racks and cool completely. Makes 15 pops.

Chocolate Chip Cookies: Drop the dough by rounded teaspoon or tablespoon. Bake for 15 to 20 minutes. Makes 40 to 80.

Prep Time: 15 minutes, plus baking time.
Kids' Steps: Measuring ingredients, dropping the dough onto cookie sheets, and inserting the sticks.

Ice-Cream Treewiches

KEEP A STASH of these treats in the freezer to satisfy a holiday sweet tooth.

Best-ever Sugar Cookie dough (see page 7), colored green
Christmas tree cookie cutter
Candy "ornaments"
Cookie Frosting (see page 15)
Half-gallon block of ice cream

Roll out the dough to ¼-inch thickness between two pieces of waxed paper. Use the cookie cutter to cut out the trees. Bake as directed.

Once cooled, attach the candy with icing to half the trees. Cut a ½-inch-thick slice off the ice-cream block and cut out ice-cream trees with the cookie cutter. Sandwich the ice-cream trees between the cookies, wrap in plastic bags, and freeze. Makes 24 Treewiches.

Prep Time: 15 minutes, plus preparing and baking the Best-ever Sugar Cookie dough.
Kids' Steps: Cutting cookie dough and ice cream with the cutters and decorating the trees.

candy ornaments for cookies

When it's time for kids to decorate Christmas cookies, the more sprinkle options you have, the better. Look for tiny candies at the grocery or candy store and buy them in small packages — variety, not quantity, is key. Here are some favorites:

* M&M's Minis and chocolate chips
* Red hots
* Skittles
* Shoestring licorice and fruit leather
* Starlight mints
* Gumdrops
* Gummy bears, fish, and stars
* Life Savers candies
* Nonpareils
* Tiny jelly beans
* Crushed hard candies
* Mini chocolate kisses
* Necco wafers
* Mini marshmallows

Pretzel Garland

INTERNATIONAL

Chocolate Pretzels

DURING THE HOLIDAYS, these charming cookies are baked in homes throughout Germany. To add authenticity, brush them with an egg-white glaze, then sprinkle with coarse decorating sugar.

2½   cups all-purpose flour
½   cup unsweetened cocoa powder
½   teaspoon salt
1   cup unsalted butter, softened
1   cup sugar
1   large egg, at room temperature
1½   teaspoons vanilla extract
1   egg white beaten with 2 teaspoons of water for glaze (**optional**)
    Coarse decorating sugar (optional; available at stores that sell cake-decorating supplies)

In a medium-size bowl, stir the flour, cocoa powder, and salt. In a large bowl, using an electric mixer set at medium-high speed, beat the butter and sugar until light and fluffy. Beat in the egg and then the vanilla extract. In three additions, beat in the flour mixture. Divide the dough in half and form each half into a log that is about 6 inches long. Wrap each log in plastic and refrigerate for 1 hour, or until firm. (It can be refrigerated overnight, but you may need to warm the dough a little bit with your hands to soften it.)

Preheat the oven to 350°. Lightly butter several baking sheets. Remove one log from the refrigerator and cut it into twelve slices that are each about ½ inch thick. On a countertop, roll each slice into a rope that is about 12 inches long. Following the photo above, form the dough into a pretzel on one of the prepared baking sheets, pressing the ends firmly onto the loop. Repeat the process with the remaining dough, leaving 1 inch between the cookies. If desired, lightly brush the cookies with the egg-white glaze and sprinkle with the coarse sugar. Bake for about 10 minutes, or until the cookies are set.

Place the baking sheet on a wire rack and cool for 2 to 4 minutes. Using a metal spatula, transfer the cookies to a wire rack and cool completely. When they're cool, store the cookies in an airtight container. Makes about 24 cookies.

Prep Time: 15 minutes, plus baking and decorating. **Kids' Steps:** Measuring ingredients, shaping the dough into pretzels, and sprinkling them with sugar.

PRETZEL GARLAND

Here's a festive and tasty addition to your Christmas tree.

**Chocolate Pretzels (recipe at left) or store-bought chocolate or white chocolate pretzels
3-foot length of ribbon**

Thread one pretzel onto the ribbon and tie one end of the ribbon to the pretzel. Weave on pretzels until the ribbon is full. Secure the ribbon to the last pretzel and hang.

Holiday Garland

COOKIE NECKLACE

With a piece of shoestring licorice, a sugar cookie can become a necklace — or an ornament for the tree. First, cut letters or holiday shapes out of cookie dough. Then punch a hole in the dough with a chopstick. Bake, then repoke the holes. Once cooled, decorate the cookies and string with licorice.

STRING THIS CHRISTMAS greeting on a mantel and it won't hang around for long!

Best-ever Sugar Cookie dough
   (see page 7)
Cookie cutters or cardboard
   patterns for the letters *A, C, E,*
   ***H, I, M, R, S, T,* and *Y* (the tops**
   of each letter should be at least
   ½ inch wide)
Chopstick
Cookie Frosting (see page 15)
Ribbon or yarn

Roll out the cookie dough and cut out the letters that spell *Merry Christmas*. Using the chopstick, punch holes in the tops of each cookie. Bake as directed. Repoke the holes after baking.

Fill a pastry bag fitted with a writer's tip with frosting. Pipe each letter with stripes, polka dots, or patterns. String the cookies on the ribbon, tie in place, and hang.

Prep Time: 15 minutes, plus preparing and baking the Best-ever Sugar Cookie dough.
Kids' Steps: Decorating the cookie letters and stringing the garland.

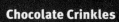
Chocolate Crinkles

Chocolate Crinkles

WHEN YOU'RE LOOKING for holiday treats to send to far-flung relatives (who also happen to be serious chocolate fans), here's a cookie that fits the bill. Rich with chocolate chips, these brownielike cookies look elegant, taste scrumptious, and travel well.

¾ cup butter, melted
½ cup unsweetened cocoa powder
1 cup sugar
2 cups all-purpose flour
1 teaspoon baking powder
1 teaspoon baking soda
½ teaspoon salt
2 large eggs
2 teaspoons vanilla extract
1 6-ounce bag semisweet chocolate chips (about 1¼ cups)
About ¾ cup confectioners' sugar for dusting

In a large bowl, mix the melted butter with the cocoa powder and sugar until well combined. In a medium-size bowl, stir the flour, baking powder, baking soda, and salt. Using an electric mixer, beat the eggs and vanilla extract into the chocolate mixture. Slowly mix in the dry ingredients until combined. Stir in the chocolate chips. Cover and refrigerate the dough for at least 2 hours or overnight.

Preheat the oven to 350°. Roll the dough into balls about 1 inch in diameter. Pour the confectioners' sugar on a plate or in a shallow bowl, then roll each ball in the sugar (a fun job for kids).

Place the balls on an ungreased baking sheet, leaving 2 inches between them (they will flatten and spread). Bake for 12 minutes, or until the cookies are set. Lay the baking sheet on a wire rack and cool for about 5 minutes; dust with more confectioners' sugar if desired. Transfer the cookies to racks to cool thoroughly. Makes 25 to 35 cookies.

Prep Time: 20 minutes, plus chilling and baking times. **Kids' Steps:** Measuring and mixing the dough, rolling the cookies into balls, and coating them with confectioners' sugar.

cookie care packages

Send season's greetings across the miles with a box of cookies. When you're choosing cookies to mail, stick with sturdy ones that don't require refrigeration. Good travelers include Giant M&M Cookie Pops (page 18), Molasses Cookies (page 37), Chocolate Pretzels (page 21), Wild Oatmeal Cookies (page 46), and Chocolate Crinkles, at left. Wrap the cooled cookies in plastic to keep them fresh, then box them up with tissue paper and unbuttered, unsalted popcorn to prevent breakage. Send the sweets first class.

Candy Cane Twists

WITH A LITTLE peppermint extract and a few squirts of red food coloring, you can turn this sugar cookie dough into sweets that look and taste like real candy canes. Once cooled, hang them on the Christmas tree for all to see and eat.

¾ cup butter, softened
1 cup sugar
1 large egg
1 teaspoon peppermint extract
½ teaspoon vanilla extract
2¼ cups all-purpose flour
Red and green food coloring

Preheat the oven to 375°. In a large bowl, cream the butter and sugar. Add the egg and beat well. Stir in the peppermint and vanilla extracts. Gradually mix in the flour until thoroughly combined.

Divide the dough in half. Color one half with red food coloring; leave the other half plain or color it green. To shape the candy canes, roll out a tablespoon of red dough and a tablespoon of plain or green until they are each 6 to 8 inches long. Twist them around each other and form into a candy cane, pinching the ends. Bake on an ungreased cookie sheet for 8 to 10 minutes, or until set but not brown. Makes about 25 twists.

Prep Time: 1 hour, plus baking. **Kids' Steps:** Measuring and mixing the dough and twisting it into candy canes.

Cookie Kids

LET YOUR KIDS dress these cookies in tie-dyed T-shirts, blue jeans, or striped miniskirts — all made out of frosting.

Best-ever Sugar Cookie dough (see page 7), chocolate or plain
Gingerbread man and woman cookie cutters
Cookie Frosting (see page 15)
Fruit leather
M&M's Minis or Skittles
Pretzels

Using the cookie cutter, cut out people from the rolled-out dough. Arrange them on an ungreased baking sheet and bend their hands or feet to give them personality. Bake as directed.

When cooled, fill a pastry bag fitted with a writer's tip with the frosting and pipe on clothes, features, hairdos, and shoes. Use the frosting to attach candy eyes and buttons, pretzel wigs, and fruit leather smiles and clothes. Makes 6 dozen kids.

Prep Time: 15 minutes, plus preparing and baking the Best-ever Sugar Cookie dough. **Kids' Steps:** Mixing and cutting the dough and dressing the cookies in sweet clothes.

Thumbprint Cookies

Thumbprint Cookies

EVERY CHRISTMAS, *FamilyFun* contributor Cynthia Caldwell and her two children make these sugar cookies filled with strawberry jelly. The recipe, which came from her grandmother's best friend, has been handed down across the generations.

1½ **cups unsalted butter, softened**
1 **cup sugar**
1 **teaspoon vanilla extract**
½ **teaspoon salt**
3½ **cups all-purpose flour**
Seedless strawberry jelly

Preheat the oven to 350°. In a large bowl, cream the butter and sugar and stir in the vanilla extract. In a medium-size bowl, mix the salt and flour. Add the flour mixture to the butter mixture until the dough is crumbly but holds together when pinched. Take a walnut-size piece of dough in one hand. With the thumb of the other hand, gently knead it three or four times. Roll the piece into a ball and place it on an ungreased cookie sheet. With your knuckle or fingertip, press a well in the center and fill with ½ teaspoon of jelly. Bake for 10 to 15 minutes. Cool and store in an airtight container. Makes about 6 dozen cookies.

Prep Time: 30 minutes, plus baking time.
Kids' Steps: Measuring ingredients, making thumbprints in the dough, and filling with jelly.

COOKIE PRINTING

Before you slide your sugar cookies or gingerbread men into the oven, invite your children to leave their stamp on the cookie dough. The following tools will let your kids make their creative marks:

* **Small, Clean Toys:** Make playful impressions.
* **Forks:** Create lines and polka dots.
* **Thumbs, Knuckles, and Fingertips:** Press wells in the cookie centers and fill with jam.
* **Plastic Pizza Cutter:** Cut out cookie puzzle pieces.
* **Potato Masher:** Stamp teeny-tiny squares.
* **Garlic Press:** Style hairdos, beards, sweaters, fur, or wool.

Hand-knit Sweaters

cookie cutter primer

* If you're just starting your cutter collection, head to a kitchen supply store and pick up the holiday essentials — Christmas trees, stars, wreaths, gingerbread men, bells, and, of course, Santa.
* For tiny sweets and appliquéd cookies like the sweaters at right, buy aspic cutters. These come in 1-inch and ½-inch sizes.
* For one-of-a-kind cookies, draw a shape onto a piece of lightweight cardboard and cut it out. Lay the template on rolled-out cookie dough and trace around it (parents only) with a knife (see below).

YOU MAY NOT have time to knit a real sweater for Christmas, but *FamilyFun* contributor Barbara Albright says you can easily warm hearts with one of these.

> **Best-ever Sugar Cookie dough (see page 7), colored**
> **Cardboard sweater pattern**
> **Aspic cookie cutters**

Roll out the colored cookie dough to a ¼-inch thickness. Set the sweater pattern on the dough. With the point of a sharp knife (parents only), cut out sweaters. Using an aspic cutter, cut out and remove shapes from each sweater. Cut out matching shapes from dough of another color and tap into place in the sweater, sealing the seams. Bake the cookies as directed. Makes about 24 sweaters.

Prep Time: 30 minutes, plus preparing and baking the Best-ever Sugar Cookie dough.
Kids' Steps: Mixing and rolling the dough and cutting out the sweater designs.

Sweet Sugarplums

SUGARPLUM FAIRIES are not the only ones who can make these no-bake treats. With dried apricots, raisins, and nuts, you too can whip them up like magic.

¾   **cup raisins**
¾   **cup dried apricots**
¾   **cup chopped dates**
¾   **cup walnuts**
1   **cup blanched almonds**
¼   **cup orange juice**
Granular or confectioners' sugar
   (optional)

In a blender or food processor, pulse the raisins, apricots, dates, walnuts, and almonds until coarse. Add the orange juice and pulse until the mixture sticks together. Roll it into 1-inch balls, then roll in sugar, if desired. To prevent sticky fingers, place in candy-paper liners. Store in an airtight container in the refrigerator. Makes 24 to 30.

Prep Time: 20 minutes. Kids' Steps:
Measuring ingredients, pulsing the fruit and nuts in the blender, and rolling the sugarplums into balls.

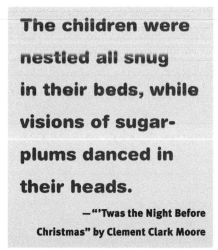

The children were nestled all snug in their beds, while visions of sugarplums danced in their heads.

—"'Twas the Night Before Christmas" by Clement Clark Moore

Cookie Swap Party

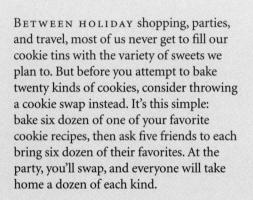

Set the mood for your Cookie Swap Party with this monster chocolate chip invitation. To make a stack of them, enlist the help of your kids in cutting "cookies" out of brown paper bags (you can use a coffee can lid as a template). Have the kids take a bite out of each cookie with a pair of crazy scissors. Next, write all the important party info on the back (or the inside, if you've made a folded card), such as the date, time, and place. For tips, see Party Planning at right.

BETWEEN HOLIDAY shopping, parties, and travel, most of us never get to fill our cookie tins with the variety of sweets we plan to. But before you attempt to bake twenty kinds of cookies, consider throwing a cookie swap instead. It's this simple: bake six dozen of one of your favorite cookie recipes, then ask five friends to each bring six dozen of their favorites. At the party, you'll swap, and everyone will take home a dozen of each kind.

Party Planning

* Invite your friends early — several weeks ahead — to give them plenty of time to dust off their favorite cookie recipes (or to try one of the recipes in this book).
* Plan the party for a Saturday or Sunday, around 3 to 5 P.M., when kids and adults are fresh from their naps and ready for milk and cookies.
* If you invite five families (for a party of six families, including your own), ask each to bring six dozen cookies. That way, everyone will get to cart home a dozen of each type. People who want to bring larger cookies should think in multiples of six (if they bring thirty-six

Giant M&M Cookie Pops, for instance, each family will get to take home six).
* Explain to your guests how the cookie swap will work: everyone will lay their cookies on a table, then pick a dozen from each plate.
* Ask each family to make copies of their recipe, enough to go around, on 8½- by 11-inch paper. Gather the recipes, and each family will have a mini cookbook to take home with the cookies.

Merry Mood-setters

* Set up a long table, draped with a table-cloth, for guests to place their cookies on when they arrive.
* Create a cookie wreath for nibbling on during the party. Arrange an assortment of cookies around a big round platter and add a red bow.
* Offer guests hot cocoa (see page 41), milk, or punch. And put out a few salty foods such as popcorn or raw veggies with dip and salsa.
* Announce a time to swap cookies. The guests are usually ready about a half hour into the party.
* End with a round of Christmas carols.

Cookie Swap Party

Rudolph the Red-nosed Cookie

reindeer cookie keeper

When he's not busy guiding Santa's sleigh, Rudolph will gladly fill up on fresh-baked goodies. To make your own Reindeer Cookie Keeper, glue a strip of brown construction paper around an empty coffee can or oatmeal container, covering the entire surface. Attach two floppy hooves and a red collar to the lower part of Rudolph's body.

To keep his ears and antlers standing tall, first tape Popsicle sticks to the backs of the cutout shapes, then tape each one to the inside rim of the container. Top it all off with Rudolph's signature feature, his shiny red nose. If you use red foil wrapping paper, you might even say it glows.

A PLATE of these reindeer cookies and a glass of milk will make Santa merry on Christmas Eve.

•

Best-ever Sugar Cookie dough
  (see page 7), chocolate or plain
3-inch-long teardrop cardboard
  pattern (for Rudolph's head)
Pretzels
Cookie Frosting (see page 15)
M&M's
Red hots

Prep Time: 15 minutes, plus preparing and baking the Best-ever Sugar Cookie dough. **Kids' Steps:** Mixing and rolling the dough and giving Rudolph antlers, eyes, and a candy nose.

Roll out the cookie dough to a ¼-inch thickness. Set the cardboard pattern on the dough. With the point of a sharp knife (parents only), cut out the reindeer's head. Bake as directed.

Let cool. Break apart the pretzels to form antlers and attach them at the top of the reindeer's head with dabs of frosting. Add M&M eyes and don't forget the red hot nose. Makes 40 cookies.

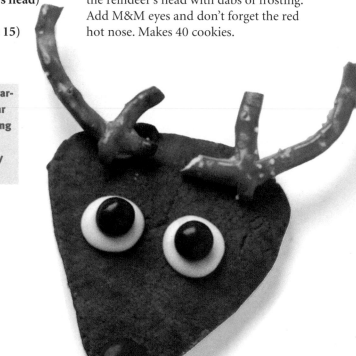

COOKIE DECORATING

Hat & Mittens

WARM UP ON A December night with an edible hat and mittens and a cup of hot cocoa.

> **Best-ever Sugar Cookie dough**
> **(see page 7), striped according to**
> **directions below**
> **Stocking hat and mitten cookie**
> **cutters or cardboard patterns**
> **Chopstick**
> **Cookie Frosting (see page 15)**
> **Shredded coconut**
> **Shoestring licorice**

Roll out the dough to a ¼-inch thickness. Use the cookie cutters to cut out a pair of mittens. Alternatively, set the cardboard pattern on the dough and with the point of a sharp knife (parents only), cut out the hat and mittens. Punch a hole with the chopstick near the corner cuff of each mitten. Bake the cookies as directed. Repoke the holes after baking. When the cookies are cool, add a coconut pom-pom to the hat with frosting and tie the mittens together with licorice. Makes 32 cookies.

Prep Time: 30 minutes, plus preparing and baking the Best-ever Sugar Cookie dough. Kids' Steps: Mixing and rolling the dough and cutting out shapes with cookie cutters.

striped sugar cookies

To make multicolored cookies, divide our Best-ever Sugar Cookie dough (see page 7) in half. Color each half with food coloring and pat it into a rectangle, about 5 by 7 inches. Wrap in plastic and refrigerate until firm. Roll each rectangle between two sheets of waxed paper until they each measure 8 by 11 inches and are ¼ inch thick. Stack on top of each other. Using a sharp, long knife (parents only), cut the dough into strips about ½ inch wide. Turn each strip on its side so that the stripes face up. Press the strips parallel to one another, alternating the colors. Place a piece of waxed paper over the strips and roll over the top to make them adhere. Cut into shapes and bake as directed.

Molasses Cookies

Molasses Cookies

HERE'S THE SNACK Old Saint Nick has been waiting for — a chewy, sugarcoated cookie that will give him a lift as he heads back up the chimney. Remind your kids to leave Santa a glass of milk as well, and a handwritten thank-you for all the gifts he leaves behind.

14	tablespoons butter
2	cups sugar, divided
⅓	cup molasses
2½	cups all purpose flour
1¼	teaspoons ground ginger
1	teaspoon cinnamon
¾	teaspoon baking soda
¼	teaspoon salt
1	large egg, lightly beaten

Preheat the oven to 350°. Cover a baking sheet with aluminum foil and set aside. In a medium-size saucepan, melt the butter over medium heat. Remove from the heat and stir in 1 cup of the sugar along with the molasses. Cool for 15 minutes, or until tepid.

Meanwhile, mix the flour, ginger, cinnamon, baking soda, and salt in a medium-size bowl. Beat the egg into the butter mixture in the saucepan, then gradually add the flour mixture and stir until well combined (the dough will be soft).

Pour the remaining sugar into a small bowl. Shape the dough into 1-inch balls, then roll each ball in the sugar. Place the balls on the foil-covered baking sheet, leaving about 1 inch between them. Bake for 10 to 12 minutes, or until the cookies have flattened. Makes approximately 5 dozen cookies.

Prep Time: 45 minutes, plus baking. **Kids' Steps:** Measuring and mixing ingredients and rolling the dough into balls.

a sweet christmas list

In a season so threatened by commercialism, time in the kitchen — cooking up sweets for everyone on your holiday list — is a balm. Besides Santa, the following folks might love to receive homemade cookies:

* Teachers
* Grandparents
* Elderly friends
* Uncles, aunts, and cousins
* Neighbors
* Baby-sitters and day-care providers
* Classmates
* Scout leaders
* Coaches
* Music teachers

Marshmallow Christmas Trees

INVITE YOUR KIDS to trim these edible Christmas trees with red hot candies.

1	**10-ounce bag large marshmallows**
6	**tablespoons butter**
	Green food coloring
6	**cups cornflakes**
½	**cup red hots**
	Nonstick cooking spray

In a saucepan over medium heat, melt the marshmallows with the butter, stirring constantly. Remove from the heat and add the green food coloring, cornflakes, and red hots, stirring well after each addition.

Once the mixture has cooled slightly, spray your hands with the cooking spray and mold cone-shaped trees, then add extra red hots. Place the trees on a waxed paper–lined tray to cool completely. Makes 12 to 18 trees.

Marshmallow Wreaths: For wreaths, form the mixture into circles and add shoestring licorice bows.

Prep Time: 20 minutes. Kids' Steps: Putting the marshmallows into the saucepan and molding the trees.

Frosty Snowmen

FIRST SNOW COOKIES

As soon as the first snow arrives, the Days, *Family Fun* readers from Littleton, Colorado, drop what they're doing and make First Snow Cookies. They begin by baking their grandma Pauline's sugar cookie recipe in snowflake shapes. Then Mom fills several small bowls with frosting and adds food coloring to get pastel colors. They frost the snowflake cookies, then add colored sugar sprinkles. Each year, the kids take on more of the cookie preparation and make the decorating more elaborate. What better excuse to make and eat cookies at 6 A.M.?

THE SECRET to these sweet snowmen is in their scarves — they're cut out of fruit leather.

> Best-ever Sugar Cookie dough (see page 7)
> Snowman cookie cutter or cardboard pattern
> Cookie Frosting (see page 15)
> Gumdrops and M&M's Minis
> Shredded coconut
> Fruit leather or shoestring licorice

Cut out snowmen from the dough and bake as directed. Once cooled, frost the cookies and add candy features and coconut snow. To form two scarves, cut a 7-inch piece of fruit leather in half lengthwise and notch the ends (or use licorice). Tie around Frosty's neck. Makes 48 3½-inch snowmen.

Prep Time: 15 minutes, plus preparing and baking the Best-ever Sugar Cookie dough.
Kids' Steps: Decorating the cookies and making the scarves.

Snowballs & Crescent Moons

Snowballs & Crescent Moons

THESE COOKIES are so delectable that many countries claim their own variations. In the United States, they're called Snowballs, but in other parts of the world they're known as Mexican wedding cakes or Russian tea cakes. The recipe is always chock-full of finely ground nuts (we use walnuts, but you could also try pecans, pistachios, almonds, or even hazelnuts). The dough can also be rolled into crescents or even stamped into stars.

1   cup butter, softened
1⅔   cups confectioners' sugar, divided
1½   teaspoons vanilla extract
2¼   cups all-purpose flour
¼   teaspoon salt
1   cup finely ground walnuts

Preheat the oven to 400°. In a medium-size bowl, cream the butter and ⅔ cup of the confectioners' sugar. Add the vanilla extract. Stir in the flour, salt, and finely ground walnuts.

To make crescents, roll a tablespoon of the dough into a 1- by 3-inch cylinder (call them "snakes" if you're working with kids). Shape and flatten the dough into a crescent. For snowballs, roll the dough into 1-inch balls. Place the balls 1 inch apart on an ungreased baking sheet. Bake the crescent moons for 10 to 12 minutes and the snowballs for 12 to 14 minutes, or until lightly browned around the edges. Cool for 2 to 4 minutes before dusting with the remaining confectioners' sugar. Once the cookies are completely cool, dust them again with sugar. Makes about 36 cookies.

Prep Time: 25 minutes, plus baking. **Kids' Steps:** Measuring and mixing the ingredients and shaping the dough.

HOT COCOA MIX

Make your own instant cocoa mix for dunking sugary cookies like the Snowballs & Crescent Moons. Measure 1⅔ cups nonfat dry milk powder, 1 cup confectioners' sugar, ⅓ cup cocoa, and ½ teaspoon salt into a plastic container or an empty coffee can. Cover and shake until mixed.

To make a cup of hot cocoa, put 4 or more heaping teaspoonfuls into a mug. Add boiling water and stir until the powder dissolves. To add a minty flavor, stir your drink with a peppermint candy stick. Makes about 20 cups.

Peanut Butter Sealed with a Kiss

THE DAY BEFORE attending a cookie swap party last Christmas, *FamilyFun* contributing editor Dorothy Foltz-Gray let her boys pick a recipe, and they both zeroed in on baking this one to bring to the party. Before they knew it, all of them were in the kitchen mixing up peanut butter dough, smooshing kisses into hot cookies, and sampling that first melted chocolate taste.

½   **cup creamy peanut butter**
½   **cup butter, softened**
½   **cup sugar, plus extra for rolling**
½   **cup firmly packed brown sugar**
1   **large egg**
1   **teaspoon vanilla extract**
1¾   **cups all-purpose flour**
½   **teaspoon salt**
1   **teaspoon baking soda**
1   **9-ounce package chocolate kisses, unwrapped**

Preheat the oven to 375°. Cream the peanut butter, butter, and sugars. Add the egg and vanilla extract. Sift the flour, salt, and baking soda together. Combine with the peanut butter mixture.

Shape the dough into 1½-inch balls and roll them in the extra white sugar. Place on an ungreased baking sheet, about 2 inches apart. Bake for 8 minutes, remove from the oven, and press a chocolate kiss into the center of each cookie. Return to the oven and bake for another 3 minutes. Cool on a wire rack. Makes 40 to 50 cookies.

Peanut Butter Cookies: For classic peanut butter cookies, roll the cookie dough into 1½-inch balls. Place on an ungreased cookie sheet and press a decoration into the dough with a fork. Bake for 10 to 12 minutes.

Prep Time: 15 minutes, plus baking. **Kids' Steps:** Rolling the dough into balls, rolling the balls in sugar, and unwrapping the kisses.

Peanut Butter Sealed with a Kiss

Chocolate Batons

Chocolate Batons

THIS SPRITZLIKE cookie comes from *FamilyFun* contributor Emily Todd. She squeezes the soft dough through a pastry or plastic bag into batons. Once baked, the cookies are dipped in melted chocolate, rolled in sprinkles, and made into a treat that gets rave reviews from all her friends.

COOKIE
1	cup butter, softened
1	cup sugar
1	large egg
1	egg yolk
2	teaspoons vanilla extract
2½	cups all-purpose flour
1	teaspoon baking powder
¼	teaspoon salt

CHOCOLATE DIP
4	ounces semisweet chocolate (squares or chocolate chips)
2	tablespoons butter
1	tablespoon milk
	Colored sprinkles or nonpareils

Preheat the oven to 350°. Lightly butter a baking sheet. In a large mixing bowl, cream the butter and sugar with an electric mixer. Add the egg and yolk, one at a time, beating well after each addition. Stir in the vanilla extract. In a medium-size bowl, stir the flour, baking powder, and salt. Gradually add the flour mixture to the butter mixture until thoroughly combined.

Spoon the cookie dough into a pastry bag fitted with a large rosette or star tip or into a ziplock plastic bag with a 1-inch opening snipped off one corner. Squeeze the dough into 2-inch-long strips on the cookie sheet. Bake for about 12 minutes, or until just lightly browned. Cool on the sheet for a few minutes and then transfer to wire racks to cool completely.

Meanwhile, prepare the chocolate dip. Melt the chocolate and butter in the top of a double boiler (the water should be hot but not boiling) or in the microwave on high, stirring every 20 seconds until smooth. Stir in the milk and remove from the heat. Dip both ends of the cookies in the chocolate, then, if desired, dip immediately into sprinkles and cool. Makes about 6 dozen batons.

Mocha Batons: Follow the recipe above, but decrease the vanilla extract to 1 teaspoon. Dissolve 1 rounded tablespoon decaffeinated instant coffee in 1 tablespoon boiling water. Add to the butter mixture after adding the vanilla extract. Add 1 tablespoon cocoa powder to the flour mixture. Bake and dip as directed.

Prep Time: 20 minutes, plus baking and dipping. **Kids' Steps:** Measuring and mixing ingredients, squeezing the dough into batons, and dipping cookies in melted chocolate.

Wild Oatmeal Cookies

FamilyFun CONTRIBUTOR Mollie Katzen found a way to please every cookie-eater in her family with one recipe. She divides the batter into bowls, one for each child, and puts out a tray of goodies (raisins, chocolate chips, chopped nuts, and dried cranberries and apricots). Then the kids go wild, adding as many or as few of these as they want to their custom cookie batches.

1½	cups butter, softened
1	cup packed light brown sugar
½	cup sugar
2	large eggs
1½	teaspoons vanilla extract
2	cups all-purpose flour
1	teaspoon baking soda
½	teaspoon salt
4½	cups rolled oats

Up to ⅓ cup dried apricots (chopped), minced walnuts, and dried cranberries or cherries (optional)
Up to ½ teaspoon cinnamon (optional)
Up to ½ cup raisins (optional)
Up to 2 cups semisweet chocolate chips (optional)

Preheat the oven to 375°. In a large mixing bowl, cream the butter and sugars. Beat in the eggs and then the vanilla extract.

Mix in the flour, baking soda, and salt and stir until "you don't see any more white," as Mollie's daughter, Eve, says. Stir in the rolled oats until well combined.

At this point, you can divide the batter into separate bowls, one for each cookie-eater. Add the optional goodies. Use some or all, in any combination. The amounts are flexible, so add as much or as little as you like, within reason. Try oatmeal-raisin-chocolate chip cookies in one bowl and apricot oaties in another. Stir as well as possible; the goodies may not be evenly distributed, but that's okay. Drop by rounded teaspoon or tablespoon onto an ungreased cookie sheet and flatten slightly. Bake for 8 to 10 minutes, or until the cookies are lightly browned on the bottom. Cool on a wire rack before eating. Store in an airtight container. Makes about 5 dozen cookies.

Prep Time: 30 minutes, plus baking. **Kids' Steps:** Measuring and mixing the dough, stirring in the goodies, and spooning the cookie dough onto the cookie sheet.

Sweet Sleigh Ride

LOAD THIS edible sleigh with chocolate candies and watch a candy dog pull it across a plate.

>   Best-ever Sugar Cookie dough (see
>   page 7)
>   Lightweight cardboard
>   Cookie Frosting (see page 15)
>   Candy canes
>   Candy cargo and a candy animal
>   Shoestring licorice

Cut out a rectangle that is about the length of a candy cane from the lightweight cardboard. Set it on the rolled-out cookie dough. With the point of a sharp knife (parents only), cut out rectangular cookies. Bake according to the recipe directions.

Once the cookies have cooled, use the frosting to attach the candy cane runners to the cookie sleigh. Pile the sleigh with candy and tie on a licorice tow rope for the candy animal. Makes about 30 cookie sleighs.

Prep Time: 30 minutes, plus preparing and baking the Best-ever Sugar Cookie dough.
Kids' Steps: Mixing and rolling the cookie dough and decorating the candy sleigh.

> Dashing through the snow, in a one-horse open sleigh. O'er the fields we go, laughing all the way.
>
> — "Jingle Bells" by James Pierpont

Santa & Heavenly Angels

SUGAR COOKIES may come in all shapes and sizes, but nothing says Merry Christmas more than cookies dressed up like Santa or a Heavenly Angel. Keep a tray of these festive sweets on hand over the holidays for hungry elves.

> Best-ever Sugar Cookie dough
>   (see page 7)
> Santa and angel cookie cutters
> Cookie Frosting (see page 15)
> Red and yellow sugar sprinkles
> M&M's or Skittles
> Fruit leather
> Yellow gumdrops
> Tiny white candy balls
> Blue gel icing

Roll out the dough until it is ¼ inch thick. Using the cookie cutters, cut the dough into Santas or angels. (If you'd like, you can also give Santa a cookie beard by pressing dough through a clean garlic press.) Bake the cookies as directed, or until they begin to brown. Cool on the baking sheets for a few minutes, then transfer the cookies to a wire rack to cool completely before decorating.

To decorate the Santa cookies, fill a pastry bag fitted with a star tip with Cookie Frosting. Pipe the icing into a full beard and use it to make Santa's hat. Sprinkle the stocking part with red sugar sprinkles, leaving the trim and pom-pom white. Use icing to attach an M&M nose and eyes and a fruit leather mouth.

To decorate the Heavenly Angels, pipe the icing through the star-tipped pastry bag into lines on the angel's gown and collar. Frost the wings, then sprinkle them with yellow sugar. Slice a yellow gumdrop into a halo and attach it to the angel's head with frosting. Attach white candy balls for the angel's buttons with frosting. For eyes, use blue gel icing. Finally, put on a red Skittles smile with icing. Makes 20 to 60 cookies, depending on the size of your cutters.

Prep Time: 15 minutes, plus preparing and baking the Best-ever Sugar Cookie dough.
Kids' Steps: Measuring and mixing the dough, cutting out the Santa and angels with cookie cutters, and decorating them with candy and frosting.

Santa & Heavenly Angels

Tasty Gift Tags

cookie presents

These Christmas cookies are a present in themselves. To make a batch, tint the Best-ever Sugar Cookie dough (see page 7) into assorted colors. Knead two colors together to create marbled cookie dough, if desired. Roll out the dough to a ¼-inch thickness. Use a knife (parents only) or a pastry wheel to cut out squares and rectangles. Bake as directed. Fill a pastry bag fitted with a writing tip with frosting, then pipe ribbons and bows onto the packages. Or, attach a shoestring licorice bow with the frosting.

PUT YOUR KIDS in charge of wrapping the Christmas presents and delivering them with these sweet gift tags.

Best-ever Sugar Cookie dough (see page 7)
Pastry wheel or sharp knife
Cookie Frosting (see page 15)
M&M's Minis and other tiny candies

Roll out the cookie dough to a ¼-inch thickness. Use the pastry wheel or knife (parents only) to cut out 3- by 4-inch rectangles. Bake as directed. Once the tags have cooled, fill a pastry bag fitted with a writer's tip with frosting. Pipe names and designs onto the cookies and add candy decorations. Makes 24 tags.

Prep Time: 15 minutes, plus preparing and baking the Best-ever Sugar Cookie dough.
Kids' Steps: Measuring and mixing the ingredients, cutting the dough with a pastry wheel, and decorating the gift tags.

Pinwheel Pops

THESE COOKIE POPS, perfect for stuffing into stockings, can also be made out of any two dough colors you like.

Best-ever Sugar Cookie dough (see page 7), plain and chocolate Lollipop or Popsicle sticks

Roll out the plain and chocolate dough separately between two sheets of waxed paper into 12- by 8-inch rectangles, about ¼ inch thick. Remove the top sheet from one rectangle; remove both sheets from the second rectangle and place it on top of the first.

Starting with one of the 12-inch sides, roll up the dough jelly-roll fashion (do not roll the waxed paper into the dough, but use it to help you roll the dough). Wrap the waxed paper around the outside of the roll and refrigerate for at least 1 hour.

Cut the roll into ½-inch-thick slices, place on an ungreased baking sheet, and insert a stick at least 1 inch into each cookie to form a pop. Bake as directed. Makes about 3 dozen pops.

Pinwheel Cookies: Skip the stick and bake these cookies on an ungreased cookie sheet.

Prep Time: 20 minutes, plus preparing and baking the Best-ever Sugar Cookie dough.
Kids' Steps: Measuring and mixing the ingredients and inserting the Popsicle sticks.

PICK UP STICKS

The hardest part about making Pinwheel Pops or the Giant M&M Cookie Pops on page 18 may be finding the Popsicle sticks, unless your kids eat Popsicles nonstop. To gather a stash, head to your local craft store and buy a bag of craft sticks (150 cost about $3). Or, hit a party or gourmet store and purchase a bag of white lollipop sticks (a bag of 50 costs about $1).

Raspberry Tarts

THESE SWEET HEARTS are a variation of the traditional Czech Linzer cookies that are popular at Christmas in Eastern Europe. The jam-filled cookie sandwiches make pretty gifts from your kitchen.

    2   heart-shaped cookie cutters
        (1 slightly larger than the
        other)
    3   cups all-purpose flour
    5   egg yolks
    1   cup butter, softened
    ½   cup plus 2 tablespoons sugar
    ½   teaspoon vanilla extract
    1   egg white, lightly beaten
    ⅓   cup ground walnuts
    1½ cups seedless raspberry jam

In a large bowl, mix the flour, egg yolks, butter, ½ cup of sugar, and vanilla extract, then knead until it forms a soft dough. Chill for 30 minutes.

On a floured surface, roll out the dough to a ⅛-inch thickness. Cut a heart for the bottom of the cookie sandwich using the larger of the two cookie cutters. For the top, cut another heart using the same cookie cutter, then cut a smaller heart in the center with the smaller cutter. Brush the tops with the egg white. Mix the walnuts with the 2 tablespoons of sugar and sprinkle on the cookie tops.

Preheat the oven to 350°. Place the cookies on an ungreased cookie sheet and bake for 10 minutes. Let cool. Spread the bottom hearts with a layer of jam and put on the tops. Makes about 26 tarts, depending on the size of the cookie cutters.

Prep Time: 1 hour, plus baking. Kids' Steps: Measuring ingredients, rolling and cutting the dough, and spreading jam on the cooled cookies.

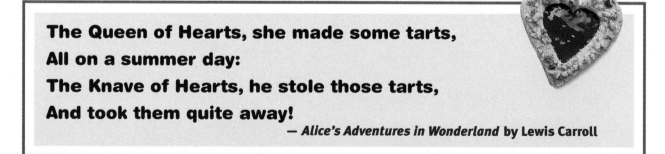

The Queen of Hearts, she made some tarts,
All on a summer day:
The Knave of Hearts, he stole those tarts,
And took them quite away!
— *Alice's Adventures in Wonderland* **by Lewis Carroll**

Raspberry Tarts

Candy Glass

Stained-glass Sweets

Candy Glass

WHEN WE RAN these directions in *Family Fun*, a host of our readers hung the results on their trees. But take note: the recipe proved to be a bit tricky. Follow the directions carefully, and the results will be a star.

> Large holiday cookie cutters,
>   at least 3 by 3 inches
> Heavy-duty aluminum foil
> Nonstick cooking spray
> Hard candy, such as Jolly Ranchers
> Colored sprinkles
> Chopstick
> 10-inch length of ribbon

For a mold, tightly wrap the bottom and outsides of a cookie cutter with foil. Set it on a baking sheet and generously coat the mold's bottom and insides with cooking spray. Fill each cookie cutter with a single layer of candies. Bake in a 350° oven for 10 minutes, or until melted. Add sprinkles, cool for 2 minutes, then use a chopstick to poke a hole near the top for hanging. When almost cool, carefully remove the foil and gently pry the candy from the mold with a sharp knife (parents only). Hang with the ribbon. Make as many as you like.

> **Prep Time: 35 minutes. Kids' Steps: Unwrapping the candies and stringing the candy ornament on the tree.**

Candy Cookies

FILL YOUR COOKIES with multicolored windows, all made out of crushed candies.

> Heavy-duty aluminum foil
> Nonstick cooking spray
> Best-ever Sugar Cookie dough
>   (see page 7)
> Round cookie cutters and aspic
>   cutters
> Chopstick
> Crushed hard candies
> Shoestring licorice or ribbon
>   (optional)

Cover a baking sheet with the foil and lightly coat with cooking spray. Roll out the cookie dough and cut out rounds. Use aspic cutters to cut out shapes within each circle. To make a hanging cookie, punch a hole in the top of each cookie with a chopstick.

Place the cookies on the baking sheet and bake as directed. Halfway through the baking time, fill the holes with the crushed candy (do not overfill). Once thoroughly baked, repoke the hole at the top of the cookie. Cool, then thread with shoestring licorice or ribbon. Makes about 3 dozen.

> **Prep Time: 15 minutes, plus preparing and baking the Best-ever Sugar Cookie dough.**
> **Kids' Steps: Measuring and mixing ingredients, cutting the dough, and crushing candy.**

Old-fashioned Shortbread

RICH AND BUTTERY shortbread is a staple in the British Isles, especially over the holidays. This recipe is made by hand, not by electric mixer, which produces a cookie with a superb texture.

2	**cups all-purpose flour**
1	**cup butter, softened**
¾	**cup confectioners' sugar**
1½	**teaspoons vanilla extract**

Preheat the oven to 350°. In a medium-size bowl, mix all the ingredients together with your fingers until the dough is smooth and holds together.

Divide the dough in half. Press each half into an ungreased 8-inch round tin (be sure to spread the dough evenly and smooth out the top). Using the tines of a fork, make a decorative border around the edges. Then, use a sharp knife (parents only) to cut the shortbread into eight wedges. Bake for 15 to 20 minutes, or until the edges begin to lightly brown.

Remove the shortbread from the oven and immediately recut the eight wedges with the sharp knife. Cool in the pan for 30 minutes, then transfer to a wire rack to cool thoroughly. Makes 16 pieces.

Prep Time: 15 minutes, plus baking. **Kids' Steps:** Measuring ingredients, mixing the dough by hand, pressing it into the pan, and decorating the border with the tines of a fork.

PASS ON A FAMILY RECIPE

When you're packing cookies for a Christmas gift, don't forget to slip in a copy of the recipe. Once the cookies disappear, your gift will keep on giving. Ask your child to copy the recipe in his neatest handwriting and include a baker's help line — your phone number — with a drawing of the finished product. If you're sending assorted cookies, tie the recipes together with a ribbon and attach a new cookie cutter.

Old-fashioned Shortbread

Home Sweet Home

Home Sweet Home

1

When the editors of *FamilyFun* invited a group of kids to decorate a gingerbread house, we knew it could be a potential disaster. The task could take hours, the kitchen could turn into a sticky mess, or worse, the gingerbread walls could cave in. So in the days leading up to the project, we did everything we could to simplify the project. The results? The kids had a great time building and nibbling on their sugar houses — and it wasn't disastrous at all. What's more, our blueprint inspired hundreds of *FamilyFun* readers to build their own Home Sweet Home.

Build the Shoe Box Frame

Most gingerbread houses require balancing a roof and four cookie walls with your fingertips, then attaching them with Royal Icing, a frosting that acts like cement when it hardens. To avoid this balancing act, we built a cardboard frame out of a shoe box and attached the cookies to it.

> Shoe box
> Graph paper
> Pen
> Scissors
> Lightweight cardboard
> Tape

2

The shoe box, turned upside down, will be the base of the house. But first, trace around one of the longer sides of the box onto a piece of graph paper and carefully cut along the lines to make the pattern for the roof. Next, trace the graph paper pattern three times onto a piece of light-weight cardboard and cut out the pieces. Tape the long side of one cardboard cutout along the top of the turned-over box; repeat with the second on the opposite side of the box. (Save the last piece to use as a template for cutting out the gingerbread dough.) Finally, tape the top edges of the cutouts together to form the triangular roof (**see step 1 at right**).

Tip: Make sure the shoe box isn't too large. We tried a box from a pair of men's soccer cleats, and the proportion of the roof pitch to the house was way off. A box from children's or women's footwear is ideal. For the lightweight cardboard roof, we used an empty pizza box, but the back of a notepad works, too.

3

> **Prep Time:** 15 minutes to build the shoe box frame, 15 minutes plus baking time to make the gingerbread, 15 minutes to prepare the Royal Icing and raise the walls, and 30 minutes to decorate the house. **Kids' Steps:** Mixing the Gingerbread Dough and the Royal Icing and decorating the house.

4

 5

 **6**

 **7**

 **8**

Bake the Cookie Walls

Gingerbread Dough

These cookie walls are not only durable, but they taste good, too. To make the project more manageable, bake the cookies the night before you plan to decorate the house.

1	cup butter, softened
1	cup brown sugar
1¼	cups molasses
2	large eggs
1	tablespoon cinnamon
1	teaspoon ground ginger
1	teaspoon salt
1	teaspoon baking soda
6	cups all-purpose flour

In an electric mixer, cream the butter and brown sugar until fluffy. Blend in the molasses, then beat in the eggs, one at a time. Add the cinnamon, ginger, salt, baking soda, and half the flour and mix well. Then add the remaining flour, 1 cup at a time, until the dough is shapable. Form into four thick pancakes; layer on waxed paper and refrigerate for at least an hour.

Preheat the oven to 350°. On a floured surface, roll out the dough to a ¼-inch thickness. Dust the cardboard template you made earlier with flour. Place it on the dough and trace around it with a sharp knife (parents only); repeat three times (**see step 2**). For the ends of the house, lay a pentagonal side of the cardboard frame on the dough and cut around it with the knife; repeat (**see step 3**). You should have four rectangular cookie cutouts (two sides and two roof pieces) as well as two pen-

tagons (two end pieces). Place the cutouts on a greased cookie sheet, checking them against the pattern again for accuracy. Bake for 10 to 15 minutes. Cool thoroughly on a wire rack. Makes 1 house, plus gingerbread trees and a gingerbread family.

Put Up the Gingerbread Siding

Royal Icing

Once the gingerbread has cooled, you can begin to assemble your house. But first, you'll need to make the icing "cement."

4	egg whites (or substitute 2 tablespoons water and 2 tablespoons Wilton meringue powder for each egg white)
6	cups confectioners' sugar
½	teaspoon cream of tartar

In an electric mixer, beat the egg whites with 1 cup of the confectioners' sugar and the cream of tartar until smooth. Add the remaining sugar, 1 cup at a time. Mix until creamy and smooth. Keep a damp cloth over the bowl to prevent hardening.

Next, place your cardboard frame on a clean work area and lay the gingerbread walls beside it. Spread the icing on the back of one piece and place it on a matching side of the cardboard house (**see steps 4 and 5**). Hold it in place for at least 1 minute, or until the frosting dries. Cover the remaining sides of the box with the cookie pieces.

Decorate the House

Now for the fun part: lay out sweets and help your kids plan a design. You might **Stack a Chimney** with vanilla and chocolate wafers, caramels, black licorice bits, or sugar cubes. **Decorate a Doorway** with a cinnamon stick frame and Chiclets gum windowpanes, red licorice and Life Savers candies, pretzel sticks and red hots, or a Life Savers candies wreath with a shoestring licorice bow. **Raise a Candy Roof** with Frosted Mini-Wheats, Necco wafers, gumdrops and licorice, gum sticks, sliced almonds, or mini crackers. **Install a Sugar Window** with sugar wafer shutters, a candy flower window box, peppermint stick panes, or icing curtains.

Now you're ready to start decorating. Fill a pastry bag fitted with a writing tip with Royal Icing (if you don't have a pastry bag, use a ziplock bag with a tiny hole cut out of a corner). Pipe the icing into the gaps between the cookie walls (**see step 6**) and decorate with mini candies. Spread the backs of the other candies with icing and attach them to the house or pipe on garlands, wreaths, and windowpanes with icing (**see step 7**).

Once you have decorated the house, place it on a large piece of cardboard covered with foil (**see step 8**). Then construct a walkway with Necco wafers, nonpareils, or Starburst candies. Build a fence with pretzel sticks and gumdrops or peppermint sticks and shoestring licorice roping. Landscape with Royal Icing icicles, confectioners' sugar snowdrifts, marshmallow snowmen, gingerbread cookie trees, spearmint leaf shrubs, and pretzel logs.

STACK A CHIMNEY

DECORATE A DOORWAY

RAISE A CANDY ROOF

INSTALL A SUGAR WINDOW

Index

ALSO FROM FamilyFun AND ⧉HYPERION

✶ **FamilyFun's Cookbook** by Deanna F. Cook and the experts at *FamilyFun*: a collection of more than 500 irresistible recipes for you and your kids, from healthy snacks to birthday cakes to dinners everyone in the family can enjoy.

✶ **FamilyFun's Crafts** by Deanna F. Cook and the experts at *FamilyFun*: a step-by-step guide to more than 500 of the best crafts and activities to do with your kids.

✶ **FamilyFun's Games on the Go** by Lisa Stiepock and the experts at *FamilyFun*: a collection of 250 great games and tips for families who travel by car, plane, or train.